You Don't Speak
My Language

Kendall Brewer

Book Cover by Kendall Brewer
First Edition, 2025

ISBN 979-8-9988289-0-4
Library of Congress Control Number 2025909098

Candlebrew Publishing
Austin, TX
Email inquiries to candlebookbrewery@gmail.com

brewer.neocities.org

Dedicated to my friends who have always loved me when I needed it most,

and to my forever person, Koby, for being the first set of eyes for everything I make.

Table of Contents

Moving Out

Cruel Love

Trapper

What's Wrong?

Only Lover For Me

Reflections

Reprieve

Seasonally Effective

Born April, 2020

A L

Wake

Cardynal (like the bird)

Now's Not A Good Time

Retreat

be safe

Come Home Before Midnight

Bow & Arrow

Price

Arbuckle Mountains

Non-Verbal

Tuning Needed

The wire strings of
instruments
grow weak and
sharp
shrill, warped metal
wound tightly for so
long around the
pegs.

They require
winding, or
else replacement
in order to be
able to release sweet
music once
again.

I wonder if, perhaps one
day I may feel content, that I
will have a day to myself,
where I do
not feel any
tension
at all.

Good Enough

Even before I was born
the doctors worried your body
would try to reject me

You did cocaine
(I have known
since I was six)
But you avoided processed meats

They let you take me home
with sensors
because my lungs did not work
They still don't

My organs glue themselves together
My brain can't focus when I read
when I think
when I do anything
"So? Everyone's got a little ADHD"
you say

You always say
that you quit smoking
while pregnant

Jigsaw

i am not a person the way you are
your body is a jigsaw
pieces fit together
each with a purpose
my body is not like yours
my body is a host
and i
a parasite

Dress Rehearsal

my body is a vessel
the same way a bottle can hold acid
it is a tool that carries me
that moves
that lives
but i do not

i exist in a different domain
like a wet shroud clinging to my body
it only exists for me
there is no touch
there is no-body
only me

my mouth is on my body
but it speaks words from a different mouth
not mine
it is not connected
not my voice
whose is it?

i am the ultimate imposter
those things didn't happen
my feelings aren't real
only if i tell someone
only if they believe me
i can't

those feelings exist only in my domain
they happened there, not here
if my domain isn't real
then my feelings aren't real
then i am not real

what happened hurts less
than if no one believed me

Achilles

Dark evening, freezing
I am repulsive meat
Man eyes hollering
Smile with a secret
I run, black wax throbbing in my breast

Things Die

things die, just like people do

when does one die:
at destruction, or at lack of life?

The Long Sleep

life has no meaning any longer
she's lost her grip on me
and when things get even harder
i lose the will to be

i yearn for a simple release
i pine so hard that i weep
i want her to wrap me in her embrace
my dearest love, the long sleep

i crave for solitude
i crave to be alone
every love in which i partake
makes me want to run, to go

i want to run until i can't breathe
where i'm sure no one can find me
i find my mistress' comfort so sweet
my darling lover, the long sleep

Louder This Time

do you feel the sharp sting?

the tired, sleepless sweat of your raw
soul?

there is no sound in the fallow poetry
of shame

Refractions

I cried to the attorney's intern
I wanted a name
one you could not call me
A name you would not recognize

I cried because
the story no longer
feels real
A lifetime ago
Yet put into words
only a handful of times
Dreamy
like reading a script for the first time
poorly rehearsed
unfamiliar
a story that is not mine

I faced wrath for poking the bruise
visited a few days later
the devil reminding me
of forgotten things
smothered, hidden away
like bed sheets soaked in urine

He dug them up
forced me to behold
memories smeared in filth

The way my nails felt against my teeth
The place you left my underwear
Nauseated silence when you finally left
leaving my broken body behind

Who's story is this?
Is it mine?
Does its lineage follow this new name?

No Feeding Necessary

solitude is a yeast

dark tar grows, consuming the rural soul

a desperate colony of morbid malaise

brewing void

Tell Me About Yourself

私はや？

巣出身です

割れた殻

watashi wa ya
su shusshin desu
wareta kara

what of me? my place
of origin is the nest...
a broken eggshell

Translation notes can be found at the end of the book.

It Follows Me

I dream at my feet there is a gorge

I have been here
so many times before
In different colors
In different forms
The edge of the earth
or along a neighborhood path

At the bottom lies
swampy water that I sink into
each footstep choked by mud
as I try to escape

Sometimes I drown in deep water
Thick reeds, algae, masking a black lake
as my feet slide out from under me where I walk
sliding down a slick slope to the water below
I look up and see sunlight
filtering down through the gaps

Or else I slink along the edges
Pebbly slopes that I must catch my footing on
clinging to trees with slim branches
My arms ache each time I slip
shoulder sockets stretched taut
I cannot keep holding on

What depth is there inside of me,
that conspires to swallow me whole?

Pity

You tell me that you love me
and I look away,
    embarrassed for you

Public Service Announcement

Shouts careened in the autumn night like arrows,
the tips soaked in cheap rum.
The house shook and quaked,
an elbow swung into drywall.
Despite the predictability,
despite the frequency the sirens sound,
I feel myself sinking like a moldy fruit,
a puddle flat on the floor.
Someone stumbles outside,
slamming the car door shut and
playing Billy Eilish at full volume.
The driver's seat will be laid back,
and the car will run all night,
until there's no more alcohol in the tank.

We now return to our regularly scheduled programming.

Rocks Against My Knees

there is dirt in my teeth
who put it there?
there are scabs on my knees
is that blood?
why is my face wet?

why didn't i scream?
why didn't i move?
it wasn't real,
that barrel pressed against my head
too many hands, too many hands
they laughed, how easily i was coerced
does it even really count?

why me?
why again?
i'm not a child anymore
this shouldn't happen anymore
i can't take this anymore

my entire body feels swollen
how long have i been here?
i wish i knew the time
five minutes, or a year?

this isn't really happening
i'm just a liar
why do i never scream?
honest people howl
why do i never move?
honest people run
only liars freeze,
headlights reflecting in their eyes

who is it that brought me here?
who moved my legs?
who silenced my throat?
was it me?
it couldn't be
i didn't want this
whose body is this, then?
it can't be mine

who am i?
who am i?
who am i?

Mercy Would Be Death

what did you think about? at night?
    did you think about me?
   what other thoughts did you think about me,
      that you only shared with God?

i wish you had thought more
         about where to discard my dead body

Reactive

I hold a squirming animal,
a creature between my hands,
a wild animal, a feral animal,
meant to be left be.

Writhing in my hands, trying to escape
Its fear is tangible in the rapid
thumpthumpthump
in its chest,
adrenaline surging beneath my fingertips.

It kicks its legs, tries to claw me,
struggling to escape, run,
gnashing fangs, flapping frantic wings
breathing rapidly,
so fast its heart may pop.

Hyper aware and lucid,
eyes darting back
and forth
seeing everything,
seeing nothing.
Too fast to process,
but seeing
nonetheless.

Acquisition

"The first step towards getting somewhere is to decide that you are not going to stay where you are."

- J.P. Morgan

Moving Out

Fresh clean carpet
stretched before a wall of glass,
projecting a box of sunshine

An eye level sunset,
creamy gold spilling
staining pink velvet

Crisp white sheets,
soft and warm,
failing body swaddled in thick duvet

Steel lock bolting the door,
a single key on the nightstand,
the only copy, and it's mine

Cruel Love

cruel love is a cage
the edges of this love,
its rules, its demands
clear and visible
it traps you in its clutches
because it is small, weak

kind love is an open field
because it knows that if it must find you
in the wide unending grass
it is strong enough to cross the distance
and greet you

Trapper

I am a big game hunter
surrounded by dangerous prey
a guilty syrup in my veins

Bear traps snap shut selfishly
beasts shipped to micro zoos
to be gawked at by perverse payers
turned on by exotic captives

What's Wrong?

"Perhaps it is depression."
"It may be narcolepsy."
"You shouldn't be this fatigued."
Always, always tired.

Only Lover For Me

Lemongrass and lavender fills the air,
intoxicating my senses.
The soft mattress fills every curve of my body,
fitting against me as if afraid to let me go,
cradling me in its embrace.
Freshly washed bedding caresses my skin,
baby blue sheets kissing my knees and shoulders.
My head sinks in the reassuring lap of my pillows,
the fan petting my hair, stroking my face.
I cannot help but succumb to the adoration,
giving myself into the safe arms of sleep.

Reflections

Perhaps a person is not a person,
but rather reflective glass
Each passerby who touches its surface
leaves smudges marring the image
And when someone looks upon it,
they will see what they want to see
and will ignore what they want to ignore
The mirror taking on the image
most suitable for the viewer
I am certain that this fact is true
because I have never looked at a mirror
and first noticed its frame.

Reprieve

Snow falling outside
There is no work today now
My bed swallows me

Seasonally Effective

Frigid, heavy, like a fallen tree
Unmoving, unspeaking
difficult to reach

My cracking branches threaten to
fall under the weight
damaging whatever lies in my path.

My freezing winds bite and snap,
fingertips that dwell too long becoming
frostbitten.

Words are lost to the bitter wind,
the arctic fields unresponsive.
The short days and long nights prompt me:

Hibernation

Born April, 2020

My cat continues to cry at my door each morning when I leave.
I worry that throughout the day, he'll continue to make a din.
Because of this occurrence, I have come to thus believe:
Between the two of us, it's me who emotionally supports him.

A L

buried eight years back
ladybug on my hand--you
are keeping watch, now

Wake

The sky outside is egg yolk,
too warm in a sticky kitchen.
My bedspread is a burial shroud,
lifeless limbs braided in the sheets.

I slip momentarily under once more,
before furiously paddling back,
struggling to claw my way to shore,
out from the ocean of fatigue.

My heavy body is wed to the mattress,
a seed refusing to sprout, to bloom
like a tulip in the dawning spring.

The sky is now cerulean,
and I am expected to already have
climbed atop the saddle;
the British would have already arrived by now.

Thumbs pressed into eyes,
red stars emerging in the dark of eyelids
like diamonds under intense heat,
a zombie finally emerges from the grave.

Cardynal (like the bird)

Eyes that never shut fully
Crying at the door each day
You cannot bear my absence
Quarantine kitten

Now's Not A Good Time

To know when it is time to speak,
I have worked hard to learn this skill,
And find myself growing weak.

Even when my heart and thoughts feel bleak,
I force myself to swallow the bitter pill,
That I must know when it is time to speak.

The words choke me like a flooded creek,
They rupture out of me when I overfill,
And find myself growing weak.

My mother's most bountiful critique,
That my selfish urges I must learn to kill,
That I must know when it is time to speak.

Even with my twin I am now meek,
His wish to drain the well, I struggle to fulfill,
And find myself growing weak.

And now I have perfected the technique,
The discipline I've worked hard to instill,
I know when it is time to speak,
Yet I still find myself growing weak.

Retreat

only some must burn from the
                          live black moss

see your own bare fear call you
                to roam home solo

        did you?

be safe

Imagine your seatbelt as my arms
I hate how fast your friend drives

Come Home Before Midnight

our home is empty without you
so quiet that i can hear
the water flowing through the pipes
and each rotation of the ceiling fan
the air cold on my skin
without you on the couch warm next to me

as i watch the front door
and stare at the patio table
where your plant pots sat
before you left

i know you will return eventually
i only wish that waiting
did not make waiting feel so long

Bow & Arrow

You laugh
and say,
"You don't know."

Victim.
It must
always be
about you.

Price

back aching sorely
new job lifting things onto shelves
enjoy your hot pot

Arbuckle Mountains

I always told you
the only way I could leave
would be in a body bag

Instead, I left with you

Fluency

Waco, TX

The hardest part isn't saying "hello"
It's not asking, "how was your day?"
Not fanning the small ember of friendship
Not finding the right things to say

The hardest part isn't the patience
It's not 2 AM, breaking down
Not trying, fighting, and pleading
Struggling to keep him around

The hardest part isn't biding your time
It's not budgeting each dollar you spend
It's not planning, packing, replanning, repacking
Or the fear it will all lead to the end

The hardest part isn't the knowing,
or the way his smile glows like a halo
It's the locked eyes, the tearful goodbyes
The hardest part is crying in Waco

Recover

Sunlight warms my face
Summer is the kind season
I am safe outside

The Painter's Sonnet

I want to show the parts of you I know;
Each passing day I hear your thoughts within,
And with each of your thoughts, I see you glow,
As does my warmth and love for you, my twin.
It grows and glows like grass in field and grove,
A fondness waters blooming garden grounds,
And beckons deer and hare to come and rove,
Where lush green sprouts thrive, and our growth abounds.
Your luminance is radiant and rich,
An endless well of my inspiring muse.
You weave ideas with mine like one would stitch,
A stroke of paint imbuing gorgeous hues.
I beg of fate for you, that you shall see,
The deep, unending love for you in me.

November

my car skid off the road
slick rain on the slope
that my tires slid across

into rotting reeds and thickets
torn under my tires
rain tapping on my roof

my eyes meet old metal tracks
deeper in the shrubs and weeds
overrun with meager moss and sprouts

another realm rests beyond the road
vivid greens rising between rotten rails
rebelling against the frigid rain

the brush springs back behind my wheels
there is no death better, as I drive,
than drawing my breath here

Zilker Park

You try to read my mind
As we watch families splash in the springs
You who's always on my mind,
Guess what color I'm thinking of

the little things

shimmering oil gloss
silky blanket, elegant sheen
starch on soft mochi

Home is with You

I hear your laughter through the walls
your cat's name sounds so much like mine

You always unload what I load
methodical and diligent
You tell me
it comes with the gig

I wrote a poem on my door
dry erase marker staining the white board
When I go to replace it you tell me no,
no
wait
You haven't taken a photo of it yet

You know when I am sleeping
because my breathing changes
in bed next to you

You speak my name
I open my eyes
the day's first words to me
"I want you to be awake now"

Baby Kitty

your cat loves my blanket
kneading it with her paws
her claws snag me in my sleep
she cries to me when you are gone
this is how i know i'm yours

(1) Unread Message

you ask why I am smiling
while I look down at my phone
but it has always been you

It's 9 o'clock

the sweetest sound known
is when you want me to wake
and murmur my name

Aboretum Stroll

You always walk in the middle of the path
You are out of reach to me,
lost in the leaves
plants are paint strokes to your eyes
Pond water mists the air
cool against my face
and I am sound carried in the breeze

We have walked a mile
I will walk so many more with you

Haiku Translation & Reading Notes

Some distinctions in the Japanese vocabulary chosen for the haiku "Tell Me About Yourself" get lost in the translation process from Japanese to English. This brief explanation is intended to touch upon some of these gaps, without necessarily explaining the poem. Like other poems in this book, the reader is still encouraged to explore the poem's meaning and find their own relationship with it.

Japanese haiku have slightly different rules and tones than English haiku. Instead of syllables, *on* are counted; in this way, "Tell Me About Yourself" follows the 5/7/5 formula.

私はや？

わ・た・し・は・や＝5

巣出身です

す・しゅ・っ・し・ん・で・す＝7

割れた殻

わ・れ・た・か・ら＝5

Additionally, traditional haiku have *kigo*, word(s) that provide a seasonal tone, and *kireji*, a word or sound to create or add a foundational tone to the poem.

The season refers not necessarily to a literal season that the poem takes place (though sometimes it does); the kigo can instead refer to a metaphorical or symbolic season. The kigo in "Tell Me About Yourself" is 巣 (su), which can mean "bird's nest." It can also refer to dens, hives, and other places where young creatures are born and/or taken care of. The season for this kigo is Spring.

The kireji for "Tell Me About Yourself" is in the first line: the や (ya) at the end. This is a unique kireji that acts as a divider in the haiku. It separates the haiku into two distinct parts, while inviting the reader to explore how these two parts are intertwined. In particular, it emphasizes the part preceding the や. Try reading the poem again, replacing the や with a long dash: "What about me?—"

If you're interested in reading the poem phonetically, here's a small chart for how to pronounce Japanese vowels. Of course, this isn't critical for the poem's interpretation, and this by no means tells you exactly how to pronounce the poem, but it will certainly be good enough for you to read it aloud to yourself.

a | yacht
i | bee
u | loop
e | red
o | crow

Additional definitions:

私は? (watashi wa) is a question, literally meaning "Me?" An example context is someone talking about their day, then asking "and you?" To which you reply rhetorically "Me?" before providing an answer about your own day.

出身 (shusshin) is a noun with complex depth. It is a noun referring to a place of origin for the subject. It has subtle connotations about their identity, by referring to the environment they come from. It is used most frequently as a noun for an immigrant or traveler to describe their home country (*Amerika shusshin desu = I come from America*); however, it is also used in contexts such as what university one graduated from, who one's family is, and organizations one used to be a part of.

殻 (kara) does not specifically refer to the shell of an egg; rather it describes shells (both egg and sea), husks, pods, and other "casings" found in the natural world. It is used in literal contexts about nature, but it is also used in figurative phrases such as the Japanese equivalent to the English phrase "come out of your shell."

Acknowledgements

You Don't Speak My Language would not be possible without a web of people in my life who have both supported my writing and just plain supported me.

Professor Kristin Hahn taught Poetry Writing at Rose State College, a course I forced myself to take because I needed to fill a limited elective. I thought that I would write some shitty poems and at least chip away at my fear of sharing my work with others, and instead I found out that I really, *really* love poetry. I was the world's worst student and turned in everything late, but Professor Hahn was right there with me still giving me just as much feedback and support as if I were a star student. Some of the poems in *You Don't Speak My Language* were written in her course, and refined with her feedback and critique. Others were written long after the course was over, because I just couldn't stop. Very genuinely, I would not have made this book without you, Professor Hahn.

At the tail-end of "Non-Verbal" I felt like I had only one close friend (we'll get to him later). Now, I am incredibly blessed to have so many that I'm going to limit myself to those who are my closest confidants.

Buzz, we have always shared a deep love for literature and media that has slowly convinced me to be literate again instead of wasting my free time on social media. You are always, always an excellent friend. Never be ashamed of the stories you love.

Jack, I am so incredibly proud of you for the progress you are making in your life. As the youngest in our group of friends, I want you to know that as you continue to become independent and to forge your path in the world, you will always, always have someone to turn to—just as I have known I can always turn to you. Your insight and your passion for my poetry projects have motivated me so much further than I would've gotten without you. I'm honored to be allowed to return the favor.

I want to acknowledge the most important family members to me: my baby brother Chris, and my "adoptive" father Darrell Wilson. Darrell, I wish so badly that you had stayed around longer. I regret that I never took the time to put into words how much your presence in my life meant to me. Of all the awful father figures I have had, you have made up for them and more. The world is more gray without you.

Finally, I would like to acknowledge my beloved, Koby. You are my eternal muse, both by inspiring me and encouraging me to continue creating, and with the stories we build and share together. I want to spend a lifetime creating art with you, and even longer admiring the art you create. You have pulled me out of my bleakest pits and you have cheered me on in my most shining spotlights. As I write this, you have been my best friend for nearly eleven years. Cheers to the many decades more ahead of us.

Author Bio

Kendall Brewer is an LGBTQ poet who graduated from Rose State College with a degree in English and achieved further education at the University of Central Oklahoma. Their poems have been published in the annual literary journal *Pegasus*, and they are a James Axley Creative Writing Award finalist and an Axley Merit Award Winner. They live in Austin, Texas with their husband Koby, cat Baby Kitty, and two ferrets. When not writing, Kendall enjoys every craft they can get their hands on, including painting, embroidery, tattooing, procedural generation, ambient music...to name a few.

You Don't Speak My Language is their literary debut. Find more at brewer.neocities.org

Content Warning Index

www.ingramcontent.com/pod-product-compliance
Lightning Source LLC
Chambersburg PA
CBHW020759130626
46554CB00006B/2271